To Marge + Dave,

Keep Choosing
LOVE + living
on Purpose.

Love,

Denise Morin

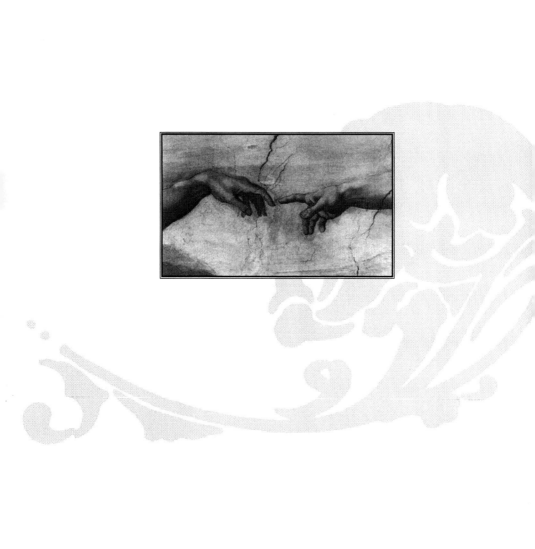

IN HONOR OF THEM

Life's Lessons
from Cancer

Denise Morin

In Honor of Them

Designed and Produced by
Maine Authors Publishing
558 Main Street, Rockland, Maine 04841
www.maineauthorspublishing.com

Contents

Foreword

I first met Denise Morin three and a half years ago. Our first connection was very powerful. We could tell from the start that we both have the same passion for our patients and their families, and for giving them what is best for them to heal. We give of ourselves, one hundred percent. This includes giving our hearts, offering our shoulders to lean on, lending our ears to listen to our patients' fears and concerns without expecting anything in return. Denise is an amazing person being able to give this gift to so many people. She is kind, loving, and giving; someone who always gives more than she ever would expect from anyone else.

Denise has a true gift of connecting with her patients and making them feel relaxed and at ease with their very first visit to the Dempsey Center. For instance, patients come in not knowing what to expect of massage. Once they have had their first sessions they feel less anxious and more relaxed, and leave wanting to come back for more. Every patient's journey is different. Denise quickly connects with each one on a different level making them and their caregivers feel at ease.

Denise also has a special spiritual sense which is unique and special not only to our patients and their families but to the Center and staff. Denise always says, "Put it out to the universe and ask." Denise is right: open your hearts, be kind, and you, too, shall receive.

I am blessed to know Denise and have her at the Center for our patients and families. She is an important part of our staff as well as a friend who is very kind and caring.

Mary Dempsey
Assistant Director/Co-Founder,
The Patrick Dempsey Center for Cancer Hope & Healing
Lewiston, Maine

Acknowledgments

First and foremost I'd like to thank God for all that He has given me: for my life, for my experiences, for using me as his instrument of love and healing.

In addition, I give thanks:

To my mother, Joan Morin, who has been the most integral part of my life as she still continues to teach me about love and the giving of self.

To my family for their constant support, uplifting spirit, laughter, and for "showing up" when I need them the most.

To my sister, Danielle Proulx, for being my "editor in chief" and for spending endless hours and energy making this book—this dream—a reality.

To my dear friend, Dinah Aldrich, for walking beside me on this road and truly believing in me.

To Chuck Davis, my friend and confidante, for his unwavering support and calming presence in my life.

To Robin Aaskov, my computer wizard and supportive friend.

And to all of you for being a part of this most special and awesome journey.

Introduction

And so, we have come to know the face of cancer. It has taken the lives of our loved ones and has left us feeling sad, angry, fearful, and lonely. It has been called the "dreaded disease." But today, I challenge you to look at cancer with new eyes. To see it as a teacher, as something from which we can learn.

This book is dedicated to all my cancer patients whom I've massaged over the past seventeen years. I have had the privilege to have comforted, loved, soothed, and listened to each one of them as most have entered their end stage of life. It is during this time that many have learned much from their illness. Their lessons while dying are here for us: to learn how to live our lives.

These are true stories. I have been beside each person and I feel this urgency to represent their "voice" and their stories. I feel them calling me to do this: to represent them.

And so let us begin this journey together.

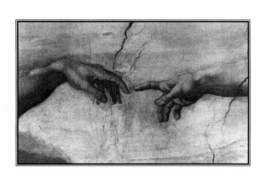

The Power of Forgiveness

Perhaps one of the greatest lessons I've learned is "The Power of Forgiveness." I learned it through Priscilla, a sixty-one-year-old mother of two who had been married for thirty-six years.

In September of 2006, Priscilla was diagnosed with a very rare form of Stage III uterine cancer. She learned of her diagnosis a year and half after her husband abruptly left the marriage. During that time she was consumed with anger and grief. You see, I believe that cancer can be activated by emotional trauma. I even wonder if it was coincidental that the cancer was found in her uterus, a place where a husband and wife can reproduce a life.

I was referred to Priscilla and provided her with massage therapy every two weeks. Not only was her body infected with cancer, her heart was filled with anger. After many honest and open conversations, we both agreed that she needed to work on forgiving her husband as a way of releasing anger's hold on her. Priscilla was receptive to this and created goals for each massage session.

She began one session by asking my help in letting go of this anger. I had her say these words with me: "Being angry no longer serves me. I release it from my body, mind, heart, and soul. I will not let my husband control me or my feelings any longer. By releasing this anger, I become healthier." During the massage, Priscilla would cry as though the anger was being released from her body through her tears.

Another session's goal was to use visualization as a tool in healing both her uterine cancer and her broken heart. Priscilla wanted to use this powerful tool to see and feel her anger actually leaving her body. She had come to learn that holding onto this negative emotion as a result of her husband's infidelity did not serve her and perhaps was, indeed, the cause of her cancer.

I honor Priscilla and respect her for looking at and re-evaluating her way of living so that she was able to overcome cancer's ill effects. This was her lesson and one we can learn from. After months of massage therapy that we did throughout her chemo and radiation treatment, Priscilla came to a forgiving spirit and, today, is cancer free!

Priscilla writes:

I've learned that forgiveness is a process. When I did the important work of forgiving someone who had hurt me, that was only the first step. Several years after my cancer treatment, I took a photography course. One week's assignment was to take pictures that would illustrate the theme of forgiveness. In completing the assignment, I realized that I had gone another layer deeper in my understanding of forgiveness. A few months later the process continued when I wrote this poem:

Forgiveness

It is arrogant pride
that darkens the tender heart
tightens the chest
and walls us off from
those we are called to love.

How easily we construct boundaries
place limits,
wallow in self-righteous indignation
and shallow justification.

One day, the heaviness
was more than I could hold.
In the darkening silence
and gifted by mysterious grace
I traded chaos for freedom,
reclaimed a part of my life
and quietly forgave us both.

(Priscilla Platt - October, 2008)

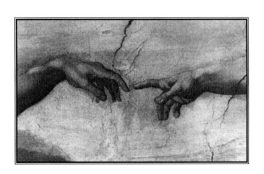

Respect

Robin taught us how important it is to respect the wishes of our dying loved ones and abide by those wishes no matter how *we* might be feeling or what *our* needs are.

Robin was married and a mother of two girls. She constantly lived her life for her family, fulfilling their needs before her own and attracting friends who needed her in much the same way. She gave of herself at the expense of her own well-being. Robin lived with breast cancer for ten years. During this time, she endured a mastectomy. If that wasn't enough, her daughter, only eighteen years old at the time, took her own life.

During our massage therapy sessions, we'd talk about life and death, and one day I asked her, "How do you do this? How do you continue to live through this suffering?" Her response was, "It's between God and me." Robin was a woman of deep faith, believing in God but also believing in her family. She had written a living will and indicated that when the time came, she did not want to be resuscitated or to be artificially kept alive.

It wasn't too long before Robin's illness progressed and her breathing became labored; she had to be rushed to a hospital. At this point, her ability to communicate with her husband and daughter was compromised. They decided to keep her hooked up to ventilators, respirators, and all the other machinery whose constant beeps were the only evidence of her being alive. They insisted that there was still hope for her. Their needs had not all been met.

I went in to see her during this time. Her body was so swollen, her eyes vacant. I could almost hear her telling me to shut it all off, to pull the plug; I knew in my heart that this was not what Robin wanted.

Her family kept her "alive" this way for three weeks, until the doctors said it was time: time to let her go.

Learn to respect and abide by the wishes of our dying loved ones.

Asking For Help

Most of us have been guilty of not asking for help when we should have, only to find out afterward that our situation would have been less stressful or painful had we done so. Don't you agree that when we share our burdens that it helps to lessen the load? I believe that often we tend to be independent to a point of sheer exhaustion or perhaps even self- induced illness.

Elizabeth had been single-handedly caring for her fifty-year-old husband, Roger, who had throat cancer. Elizabeth worked 24/7 providing for all of Roger's health needs. He had a huge tumor on the side of his neck. It just kept growing to the point where he was not even able to speak.

When I would go to their home to massage Roger, Elizabeth would be there tending his neck wound with sterile gauze in an attempt to cover it and the odor it emitted. There came a time when Roger's condition required more than what his wife was capable of providing but because she was "in it" so deeply with him, she was not able to recognize that.

I was, however, able to convince Elizabeth to admit Roger to hospice care. The doctor there had never seen a tumor quite like Roger's in all his thirty-five years of experience. He explained to us the progression of this type of tumor. Already, it had grown to the point where maggots were growing from it, and that if these were to mature to become flies, the hospice center would have to provide a light box serving to attract these flies so that Roger would not choke to death on them. I understand this might be graphic. Barbaric even. It is. But this is cancer…and this continued for six more weeks before he died.

Elizabeth suffered a stroke the following week and now lives a debilitated life.

The lesson here is to know when it is time to ask for and accept help.

Courage To Die

Have you ever encountered someone who had true courage? One who was unyielding in the face of severe adversity? Someone whose strength of character—backbone, if you will—and positive mental state enabled them to continue to live with dignity and integrity? They found a way not to be a victim; instead, they remain true to the person who they are.

Annette, at the age of thirty-seven, was diagnosed with Stage IV colon cancer. Her husband, Steve, was diagnosed with Stage III brain cancer a year later and both were seeking treatment simultaneously. Annette and Steve had two young girls, ages three and eight.

Annette was the type of person who did it all: she did everything to keep their home well managed, she took her girls skiing and snowboarding, bicycling and hiking. She, too, was physically active.

She even held onto a full-time job. She had remarked to me that her job outside of her home was particularly stressful and confided in me that perhaps it was the cause of her cancer. Annette was determined to beat this cancer. She maintained her physical activity even on those days she was not feeling well. She kept her upbeat attitude as she didn't want to worry her girls.

Annette remained so strong for another four years until she had to be cared for in a hospice setting. When she knew time was short, she asked me to do something she wished she could do but no longer could. She asked me to take her husband shopping for a blue suit (her favorite color) to wear at her funeral. So Steve and I went to the mall and got him a blue suit coat with matching shirt and tie, socks to match, even a pair of new shoes. When we returned to Annette's hospice room, Steve went into her bathroom to try on his new clothes for her. When he came out all dressed up, she squinted her eyes to see and whispered in a tired breath, "perfect…just perfect!" And smiled.

Annette was that person of true courage. She found the calm in the middle of the storm.

Annette Laneuville's Eulogy

I was honored to deliver the following words at Annette's memorial service.

I'd first like to extend my deepest sympathies to Steve, Annette's husband. You were there every step of the way, never giving up or complaining, showing Annette your unconditional love as she would say to me that Steve doesn't give himself enough credit for all that he has done for me. Annette truly appreciated your support and constant love.

To Stephanie and Chloe, Annette and Steve's young daughters whom she'll miss forever. She knew that you were both going to be taken care of. How she loved you from deep within her soul.

To Annette's mom, Doris, who was her backbone, constant support, and babysitter, and who helped Annette with whatever was needed in each moment.

To Annette's neighbors and friends, you made her feel so loved with your generous acts of kindness and caring.

And to the rest of Annette's family members, she'd want me to thank you all.

This is a sad day, indeed. Too young…too short of a life.

My name is Denise Morin and I was honored to be Annette's massage therapist and friend for two years.

Annette's essence was that of strength, a strength from her that you could feel just by being near her. Annette never complained. She even worked throughout her treatments of chemo and radiation.

Annette had endured major surgeries and suffering. She knew her final days were close.

On July 18, as I massaged her body, she said that she was tired, so tired, and knew how people felt now, and was ready to meet Jesus. I could help out so much more from heaven, she shared, than I could now. She said, "I know that Steve will be okay, and that the kids will be taken care of."

She was truly ready to let go and let God.

Reality of the finality was here, was now.

Annette taught me so much about life and about death. She taught me to be strong and to never give up, to let go of control when you no longer could control everything. She showed me how to die with integrity and dignity.

She left her caring mark on everyone, including me. At the end of our phone conversations she would always say, "bye-bye." This is not "bye-bye" but "until we meet again in heaven, my wonderful friend."

> I love you, Annette; we will forever be connected.
> Thank you Annette for "touching" my life.
> Denise Morin

P.S. I know the moment you took your last breath that God welcomed you in His arms. The next one to greet you there with a big smile and a warm hug was your dad. I know you loved him so much and missed him so. You told me that you saw shadows of him in the hospital by your bedside.

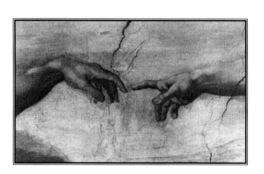

Courage To Live

An Interview with Steve Dwinal
(husband of Annette Laneuville, and a Desert Storm veteran)

How have you survived all of this?

I do it for my girls. Annette told me to be strong and take care of the girls. She whispered that in my ear in Hospice. She told me that I was a good husband and that she wouldn't change a thing. Everything that she went through—she wouldn't change a thing. I asked her to forgive me for all the bad things that I had done, and she said, "I forgave you a long time ago."

She said God chose you to take care of the kids.

I told her that I'd do my best.

Before she passed I told Annette, "Go ahead, you can go now." Then I went home and tried to keep busy. One hour later I got the call…that Annette had passed away. The girls were in school. I dropped to my knees and cried out loudly and barely could drive myself there. My parents had to physically carry me to her bedside. And I gave her my last hug.

I know I told the kids about Mommy's passing but I don't remember how I told them.

But I did say Mommy wasn't suffering anymore. I lost my soul.

Annette was my soul mate.

Who did you turn to for help?

A lady named Denise. Denise was Annette's angel and she loved Denise and her massages. She would take the day off for her massages. She would tell me how Denise was her special angel. You two were very close.

How did you get over the loneliness of it all?

I don't. I try to date. I am still functioning fully. But I tell them what I have and they get scared. That's why I don't date. They treat you like a leper. The only people who understand are people that have it.

I even have problems with family members. They don't understand because they don't have it. They don't know what you are going through.

So how do they react to you?

They complain about the house I bought and how I spoil my kids. I tell them, don't complain about it, HELP ME! I almost estranged myself from my father and sister.

They give me a lot of stress. They don't understand. They are causing me stress.

What you want to do: keep humor in your life. Watch comedy shows and start laughing. That's what Annette taught me. Annette did that every night. She always watched comedy shows and she would say it takes the pain away. Laughter is the best medicine and it is free. Do stuff that you like to do. Hunting, fishing. And what does that do for you? It makes you happy.

BE WHO YOU ARE, NOT WHAT PEOPLE WANT YOU TO BE.

Cancer is going to change your life. It makes you a better person. You try harder to become a better person because you know you could die at any time. I started volunteering at the Patrick Dempsey Cancer Hope & Healing Center. You think more about others than yourself. You believe in God more. You definitely want to be on His side!

You will have thoughts of not wanting to be alive. There will be days like that. It's not all happy days. You just have to take it day to day. Just get through the day. I have thoughts of that a lot. I wish I had been taken first. I don't know why God chose me to be alive, but He is helping me to take care of my girls.

I have sleepless nights. Do I want to wake up or not want to wake up?

Grace

Shirley was in her mid-fifties and never complained about her peritoneal/abdominal cancer. She was a highly-respected teacher in the area and one of the nicest women I had ever massaged.

She would have horrific side effects from her chemotherapy which forced her to take hot baths, sometimes at two a.m., to relieve her excruciating rectal pain.

When I entered the room, Shirley always asked about me. I would just shake my head and say to myself, how can she be asking about me when she is in such pain and agony? She was that kind of person, one who could remove herself from her own situation.

Shirley was not about herself or her cancer. She lived her life in a state of grace.

After what was to be her last massage session with me, she asked to be taken up to her bedroom, which was up some steep flights of stairs. She was determined, so I literally held onto her as we climbed each individual stair together. Her swollen, fluid-filled legs were heavy with each step. Once we got to her room, I lifted her legs up and into bed, taking each tenderly and gently placing it in a comfortable position. Exhausted from the climb, Shirley closed her eyes and immediately fell asleep.

I felt as though I had been asked to transport her to her final destination: upward…toward heaven!

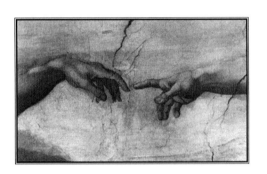

Denial

Olivia was completely in denial concerning her imminent death. She kept repeating that she was going to beat this and that she was okay, that she had more living to do! She wanted to see one of her grandchildren graduate from high school the following June and then from college four years after that. The sad reality was that she weighed only eighty pounds at this time and was hooked up to oxygen and morphine.

It may have been the time to talk with her son and daughter about important decisions but because of her denial, she never did. She never took the opportunity to talk heart-to-heart, to share her love for them, to express her wishes and desires in these final stages of her life. She stayed in this state of denial until her last breath.

Her son and daughter were not in denial and it was difficult for them to try to talk around the subject of dying with their mother. They told me that they wished she would have accepted what was going on in order to move forward together, to be on the same page, and to help each other go through this end stage of life as a family unit.

You Are Needed

If we allow it, cancer can teach *us* about *our* priorities in life.

Brian had lung cancer. He never complained or asked for much. He was in and out of the hospital many times. One night, I visited Brian there and while I was massaging him, he sat right up and said, "I wish I could see my daughter. I wish she would come over to see me." I had never seen Brian cry until that moment.

You see, Brian's daughter had never shown up for any of his hospital stays. She had told him she couldn't see him this way, that she couldn't handle it. Brian simply wanted to see his daughter; she meant so much to him.

We must learn that this is not about *us*. This is about our loved ones.

I ask you, *please* get out of your own way and be there for them. They need you!

Walk the Talk

Albion was a seventy-six-year-year old man who suffered through many types of cancer—prostate, skin, leukemia—and yet he never chose to be the victim of any of them despite the trials of surgery, chemotherapy, and transfusions. He was the most faith-filled man I had ever encountered. He allowed God to take over for him. When things became more difficult, Albion was able to bring an attitude of calmness to it, smiling and saying, "It's in the Lord's hands." He truly walked his talk.

In the end, when he was actively dying, he sat up from his living room hospital bed and asked for his bible. With his eyes closed, he opened it and started preaching from it. He knew the verses by heart and started to speak, as though to a crowd, loudly and emphatically. Those of us with him stood in awe!

And just as I am writing these words, the skies have opened up with down-pouring rain, loud bursts of thunder and lighting, and hail (on this late April day)!

Coincidence?

I think not.

Just another sign from one of my cancer patients telling me to do this: to get these words out and share them with the world. These people and their stories continue to teach us lessons.

I just sat there and smiled.

Al Rowe's Celebration of Life

(From My Eulogy)

Hello, my name is Denise Morin. I was honored and blessed to have been Al's massage therapist and friend since February.

I'd first like to extend my deepest sympathies to Charlotte. You were Al's backbone, walking every step with him, moment to moment, in total support and unending love.

To Pam, how you made Al feel so comfortable in the end, a true angel of comfort. To Diane, Linda, Wendy, and Becky for being there when Al needed you the most, and to the rest of the family: I embrace you in light, healing, and love.

Al was a faith-filled man, always leaning on the Lord in good times and in difficult times. Al taught me about courage. He never asked, "Why me?" when he got diagnosed with cancer. Instead he said, "Why not me?"

He never once complained about his many treatments, hospital stays, transfusions, or discomfort.

I recently asked him if any good can come from cancer and his reply was, "Fellowship. It gave me the opportunity to enjoy fellowship with others."

I asked him what he wanted me to share with all of you; his response was, "To keep your eyes on the Lord as He is the most steady."

Al's essence was that of caring. He always did for others and thought of others before himself. I feel his greatest purpose on earth was how he put love into action every minute of every day. I could picture the Lord as he embraced Al into His arms whispering to him: My good and faithful son!

Al could see the beauty in nature, the many miracles. He would point to the maple tree in front of his house and say there isn't one leaf that is the same. Just think about that.

Nature to him was like Heaven on earth. He loved spending time in it!

I want to thank you, Al, for being the greatest role model of service to others and for loving us like you did! I believe that we will remain connected forever in that same light and love that the good Lord is providing you with in this very moment!

Just a Bend in the Road

In my work I sometimes massage cancer patients in the Chemo-therapy Infusion Center. One day this woman told me about something that happened when she was five years old. She had been riding her Big Wheel and got hit by a car and was dragged underneath the car for some time.

She came out of it but had severe damage to her leg. Her lower leg was totally damaged and deformed. (When she lifted her pant leg to show me, it took my breath away…it did not look like a leg at all.) Her doctor told her she would never walk again. And when she later walked in front of him she remembers him crying aloud in front of her. He had big tears in his eyes, she said.

Today, she has breast cancer and has such an upbeat and uplifting attitude. "I developed this attitude and inner strength from that bad experience when I was five years old. It is just a bend in the road. This is just a bend in the road."

Stay Centered in Love

Nineteen-year-old Amelia was in her second year of college when she discovered she had Hodgkin's lymphoma (cancer of lymph tissue often found in the lymph nodes of the neck or chest). She and her family were devastated by this diagnosis.

Her mom, a schoolteacher at the time, took time off from teaching to be with her daughter. It was Amelia's dad who set up the appointment for her to receive massage therapy. During her first massage, Amelia asked all kinds of questions about how to deal with cancer. Like most, she began losing her beautiful hair to chemotherapy. At one point asked me to pull out the rest of her straggly hair as it was falling out, she wanted to get through this as fast as she could.

Amelia had tremendous support throughout her six-month journey. Once she returned to college, however, things were not the same.

Here's a letter she emailed me, which she has given permission to share:

Hey Denise

I'm really upset right now, and I was thinking of talking to someone who gets it, and I thought of you.

I've been on this website called Planet Cancer too much tonight. It makes me feel relieved that there are other people saying what I feel, but it makes me "so sad" that other people have to go through this, too.

I'm having a hard day, I guess. Just emotional. Overwhelmed.

I'm having really bad dreams the past four nights, every night I dream about death and scary stuff and wake up with my heart racing and need to cry. I have no idea what's going on. It's so bad.

I feel so bad right now, I can't stop crying and I don't know what it is. I can't explain any of it; I don't know my own feelings. I just know it's still so freaking hard.

My roommate hugged me for a while and we read some of the stuff on Planet Cancer together, but I need to figure this out on my own. I don't know what any of it is. I'm just so sad.

I feel like I need someone like you right now, someone who gets it. And I hate that expression, but I really am having a shitty time right now. It just all hurts so bad.

Someone wrote this on the website:

"I feel sick to my stomach thinking about it. All of it. Everything. I hate it. All. And I really despise when people, particularly family and close friends actually think they have the 'right' to decide 'for me' when I 'should be over it.' My heart is in so much pain at this moment. I'm not over it. I'm not over 'it.' It broke me. And I'm still broken."

I feel like I'm still broken. And always will be.

Someone else said, "But it seems sometimes that surviving cancer is harder than having it. I think I was so caught up during treatment with fighting it and there were so many people supporting me that now I feel like no one understands that this is the hard part."

The hard part.

I just feel so sad. Generally, I have been doing well, with spurts of sadness. But tonight's really bad.

I miss you and I hope you're doing well. I owe you the biggest thank-you for everything you did for me.

Love,

Amelia

I'm better. I just know I still have all these feelings and I'm pushing them away until they come back...but I don't know what else to do. It's hard but I'll figure it out. I am going on retreat in a couple weekends to Philly with young adult cancer survivors ages 18-25, so that'll be good.

I responded, "Just be in your feelings…feel them…it is okay… they'll come and go…people will understand, and if they don't, they are not your support team members! I think that retreat will do you some good! Stay centered in love."

Amelia is doing well and has a new boyfriend in college who is wonderful. He understands her, listens to her, and is health-conscious. School continues to be difficult but she manages well. This year she joined a support group with ten other adult women who have or have had cancer. That is so helpful to her.

She just found out one of her middle school friends has cancer. She writes, "It's hard talking to her and reliving it all, but it's good to know that I can help in some way."

The Boy with the Connected Touch

Alex was a twelve-year-old boy who suffered from a form of blood cancer more typically known as leukemia. He was an old soul, as he was much wiser than his age.

Alex lived with his forty-two-year old dad who, himself, struggled with Young-Onset Parkinson's disease. The two of them were inseparable, spending time together and sharing in a common belief. They believed, as Native Americans do, that being in tune with nature has healing benefits. Every time I went to their home to massage Alex, they had meditative Native American music playing while candles and incense burned beside a tabletop filled with bottles of prescription medications.

Alex's last days were spent hospitalized and in a coma. His dad called me to massage Alex. I knew when I touched his young body that Alex could feel me—a familiar touch. I could sense that he was experiencing a good feeling. All the while his brother, mother, father, and grandparents were trying to make sense of it all and trembling with fear of the unknown. I gave Alex a full-body massage in much the same way as I always had, but this time I could feel him giving back to me. I felt him thanking me without the use of words. There seems to be an unspoken connection when one shares in the intimacy of life's last moments.

In the words of Alex's father, Steve Sasseville

Many young boys play cowboys and Indians, policemen and firemen, or athlete and astronaut. This stage is often defined by its external demonstration of control or being "in charge," and offers very little internal awareness of anything beyond one's world. The child is, as he/she believes, the center of their universe. This testimony is offered in memory of my son, Alexander "Alex" Sasseville, who not only captured his dad's heart, but brought peace and acceptance to all who crossed his path.

Alex lived his brief, yet inspired, thirteen years as a student of love and unassuming acceptance. He had a fascinating understanding of the "interconnectedness" (my word, not his) of life, people, animals, birds, spirituality, the moon-sky-earth, laughing, touch, healing, and eventually, his own divinity. Children often waver from wanting to be a famous entertainer, to being a popular athlete, to being perhaps the next teen idol. Alex, however, wavered between being an architect, an animal trainer, a chef, and a massage therapist. Since the age of five, Alex always included massage therapy as a cornerstone of not only his career choice, but also as a major piece of his overall health. I know it may sound suspicious after all we've been through, and within the context of this testimonial, but the truth is Alex believed in, understood, and requested the therapeutic effects of massage for many years before it became his solace and ultimate comfort.

Alex was diagnosed with Acute Myeloid Leukemia (AML) in May of 2001. This journey that his mom, his brother, and I joined him on was one of shock, sadness, hope, disillusionment, frustration, and "connectedness." However, Alex, our ultimate teacher, gave us two years to recover, reflect, ponder, pray, and recognize the gift our son was giving us. He lived his truth. Throughout his experience, whether during his many infections and isolations in Portland, Maine or during his bone marrow transplant and subsequent multitude of agonizing and often excruciating months in Boston, Massachusetts, Alex maintained an inspired sense of peace, clarity, love, and "connectedness."

Alex was ecumenical in spirit and practical throughout his life. Whether going to bed by himself when he was three years old saying, "I need my rest, Dad. It good for me" to often saying at five years old, "No

Pepsi, Dad. I'll have some water," and always being a student of therapeutic touch. Alex was introduced to informal massage through his mom and me during his early (0-5) years and welcomed his first "real" massage at five years of age. I remember him saying, after his first experience, that he liked it a lot, but she (the therapist) "could've tickled less and been a little firmer." Over the next few years, massage, polarity, homeopathy, Reiki, became a solid and consistent part of Alex's life. As his Dad, I always wanted my children to try something before dismissing it. Then they could choose whether to include it in their lives. However, Alex and his brother have been guided to appreciate balance, embrace opportunity, and be grateful for the creator's love.

Alex not only enjoyed the physical soothing sensation of massage, but I was amazed to witness a boy of 6-7-8 relating to the internal sense of integration (my word) it offered. He would say things like, "You know Dad, after my massage I feel so calm and relaxed inside, it helps me think easier" and "Is it time for my next massage yet?"

At eight years of age, he began changing some of his career choices, but for the rest of his life, he maintained his unwavering desire to be a part-time massage therapist "in the morning," so he could take care of his dogs, cats, and horses in the afternoon and enjoy his evenings as a dessert chef and artist. Of course, Alex was sure to tell me that his "jobs" would be part-time because he was going to be "a full-time dad and husband."

Alex was often heard at family gatherings saying to someone, "Your shoulders and neck look tense; would you like a massage?" Playing along, most people would accommodate. However by the end of the rather formalized thirty to forty minute session, many often applauded his effort and especially commented on his "therapeutic touch."

Although we may all have the ability, some have developed their connectedness to a level that can be projected and felt by others as penetrating, soothing, healing warmth that begins the healing process. Alex possessed this gift, which radiated from his heart and core.

Cancer was, of course, frightening, destabilizing, consuming, and unmasking. However, Alex never made the cancer his enemy, he never battled with it, and he never blamed God or anyone for his situation. Instead, as he said to me in Boston while suffering greatly, "I was scared *the first month after I was diagnosed, but then I knew I'd be okay, Dad, because God is with me." He not only embraced his challenge, but turned it into grace incarnate. He utilized several practical methods to maintain his balance, and to endure all that was given to him. While the scientific and medical communities have now begun to recognize the comforting, calming, and healing power of touch (massage), Alex had intuitively understood this years before.*

During Alex's two to four years of intense attack on his body, he requested, coordinated, and absolutely knew the need for ongoing massage therapy, polarity, Reiki, many, many foot rubs (which were equally therapeutic for Dad), and an environment (in the hospital, as well as home) filled with healing musical vibrations, soothing aromas, comforting possessions, and gentle, calming, loving individuals.

After recognizing the debilitating and chronic condition Alex had gotten to in Boston, he and I agreed that home was absolutely the only place to be for the rest of the journey. As I prepared our home and Alex's room, organized the chaotic, yet necessary medical schedule, created a loving, antiseptic, safe setting, I knew part of Alex's therapeutic schedule needed to include massage. But with the many outings to Scarborough and Portland, Maine every week, the schedule literally did not permit another outing. Mary, Jesus, and the Creator were used to hearing from me by now, but never for anything specific, only for peace and comfort and for "Thy will be done." I placed my son in Their hands.

Several years before, I had participated in a massage workshop as a client and met a past schoolmate who was traveling the countryside doing massage therapy. I had found it to be an intriguing concept, but never gave it much thought. As I was browsing through a paper, synchronicity jumped out at me: a familiar name was in front of me, but I was concerned with the financial aspect, availability, willingness, comfort level, etc. The seed had been planted years ago, now this beautiful flower was in Alex's and my garden.

I spoke to Alex, who approved my calling this person. As I was listening on the phone, I heard a kind and sensitive voice that immediately was warm and receptive. I knew immediately, in my heart, I was connecting with the right person. Her name was Denise Morin. She listened to our story, offering knowledgeable and insightful observations, and took an active interest not only in Alex's condition, but took time to ask me about Alex as a person. I remember clearly her fascination in his Indian spirituality, love of animals, and artistic ability. She was real, she cared, and Denise clearly understood that the therapy and healing starts long before the actual physical touch.

The true test, if you will, was the Alex factor. Alex had experienced many therapists, different styles, and a host of personalities in over eight years of receiving (and giving) massages. Alex knew, especially now with his heightened physical sensitivity, the difference between a truly connected, healing massage and an "it's a job" massage. And anyone knowing Alex knew his level, respectful, yet penetrating candor.

Not only was Denise able to come to our home, saving Alex energy and allowing him to thoroughly let go, but she was generous in her financial scale, and gave above and beyond the call. Seeing Denise every week became a light of anticipated comfort and deep cellular relaxation for Alex, and her smile and kind words gave me encouragement and comfort for my unending role as a dad. Denise's business name, Connected Touch, only begins to capture the essence of what she brought to our home. Massage, of course, was the primary intention, but love, compassion, and presence were the real gifts that stayed with Alex and I long after Denise would drive away.

Alex passed over to the hands of the Creator on June 26, 2003, but the week before, after receiving his regular massage, he said, "Dad, I really like Denise. She is a very good massage therapist; her touch is deep and gentle, but you know what, Dad? I really like that she listens to me. I think she really understands what I talk about." And then he added, "Thanks Dad. It really helps to have her."

Connected Touch is about a gifted individual living her faith in a practical, loving, effective, and healing approach. Her ability as a massage therapist is unquestioned, her caring style and sensitivity creates an environment receptive to the healing life forces, and her genuine life choices reflect the sincerity of her dedication to offering a "connected touch."

Thank you, Alex, for making all this possible. Love, Pops

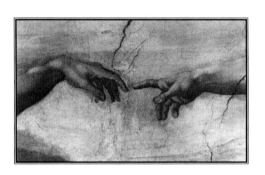

What to Do and Say

Too often we miss an opportunity to learn about life because we are fearful or are not familiar enough. And so it is with death: we don't know what to do or say to one who's dying, even if it is someone dear to us.

My best friend's mom was recently taken off dialysis and transported to a hospice home. Her entire family was there in the room with her when I arrived. Even before I entered the room, I could hear the TV's volume up really loud. The family was watching a Tiger Woods golf tournament and had to speak even louder than the TV's volume just to be heard. All while their mother was in the bed there, beside them, dying.

So, I asked them if they would turn off the TV and join me at their mom's bedside. I invited each of them to put their hands on their mother's body and if they so chose, to share some words, as this was the time.

Her children each said how much they loved her and thanked her for all that she was to them. Some said a prayer while others just broke down and cried.

It was a most powerful show of love for both the children and their mom. She died in complete peace surrounded by so much love.

Cancer teaches us what to do and what to say, *if* we are open to it.

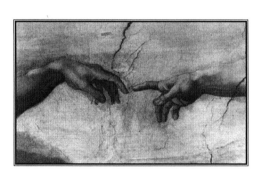

Simple Ways to Reach Out

Instead of asking a cancer patient, "How are you?" try showing your concern by asking, "Is there anything you need?" or "Is there anything I can do for you?" "Is there anyone you'd like to see?"

Or ask, "What can I do for you right now?" "What can I do to help ease your pain?"

Hold their hand. Touch them. Listen to them. (That's the biggest one!)

Or simply state, "You're in a lot of people's thoughts and prayers." Or, "I send you only positive, healing energy. It's okay to lean on me."

There's no need to fill the quietness with your words. Wait for them to talk. Treat them normally. How they crave normalcy!

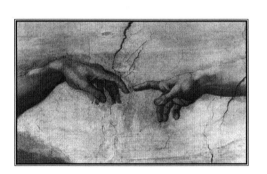

How to Be Present

Michelle, at age sixty-one, courageously battled ovarian cancer. Her family was her greatest support. Her eighty-eight-year-old mom, her three sisters, and her two brothers were constantly at her side. Their daily commitment and dedication was incredible! They took time off from their full-time jobs and families, and one sister literally moved back to Maine from Maryland for a month or so to be with her.

The family told me that Michelle was never much into being touched, so they were all so surprised at how quickly Michelle felt comfortable with me and the massages. She looked forward to our time and massage sessions together and it made her family happy to witness this special connection, as I grew close to the family as well.

Michelle spent her last days in hospice care and on her last day and night one of her sisters went into bed with her to spoon her and hold her. It was the most beautiful gesture of love that I have ever witnessed in my life.

And she died in content peace and love from her most special family.

The lesson here is that her family was truly present in every moment with her, both in the hospital and in the hospice home. They would sit by her in a circle and whenever she needed anything one of them would get up and give it to her. They participated as the entire family. It wasn't just a few of them, it was everyone all the time. I usually do not experience that with families; it was powerful. And when we all had to leave the room, we would join together in the lounge and they would all talk and reminisce about their sister and daughter. They would include me in on everything and made me feel like one of their own. To be fully present for days and months on end was a beautiful gift to each other.

The Most Important Things to Do When Someone is Dying

Visit them.

Call them.

Listen to them.

Touch them.

Ask them if there is anything they need.

Ask them if there is someone they would like to see.

Ask if you can bring them anything.

Talk to them about dying.

Let them teach you about what they are going through.

Massage their feet with lotion. (100% of my patients love to have their feet rubbed. You cannot hurt them with touch and you cannot catch cancer.)

Kiss them.

Love them up. They need that now more than ever.

Play soft music. Bring in their favorite CDs.

Put up posters or pictures of meaning on their walls.

Put the "No Visitors" sign on their door so you all can rest.

Turn off your cell phones.

Keep the room quiet and peaceful.

Keep distractions to a minimum.

Go out into the hall to talk about the patient. They can hear your every word!

When you are in the room, focus only on the patient. The other things can wait. Focused time and attention is of the essence!

Pray.

Sing.

And it's okay to laugh!

But most importantly, listen!

Treat the patient as you would want to be treated: with respect!

My Question—Their Answer

Having massaged cancer patients for over seventeen years, I can't help but ask questions, like, "How do these people go on living when they know they are dying?"

Trevor has been suffering from throat cancer for seven years. He has a tracheotomy and a feeding tube in his stomach. He is constantly coughing up heavy mucus, never knowing if he will choke himself to death during those repeated episodes. And yet, Trevor strives to live a normal life doing just about everything you and I do. His own beliefs keep him going, as he believes his life still has a purpose.

I was introduced to two brothers, seventy-year-old Bob and his older brother, Maurice, seventy-two years of age. Here are two brothers who not only share a biological heritage but, unfortunately, share the dreaded disease of cancer. Bob was diagnosed with breast cancer, Moe with renal cancer that had already metastasized to his bone and brain. How do they live, knowing they are dying? They tell me they are truly living in each moment, as that is all they have.

They cry often, speaking of leaving one another. Bob says, "I'm losing my brother, but he's losing all of us!" Moe accepts his destiny with integrity and just keeps doing the best he can.

Moe died in September of 2010 and died as he had lived: with love and dignity. He made everyone laugh when he could hardly speak. Once while I was massaging him, I said, "Moe there isn't a bad bone in your body."

And do you know what he said to that? With dry lips, after not eating or drinking for two weeks, he said, "You just haven't found it yet!"

Sharon is one who responds to this question in a way I admire. She knows that her pancreatic cancer is incurable and yet she says she lives the best way she knows how. You see, sixty-seven-year-old Sharon lives with her eighty-eight-year old mother and Sharon's eighty-two-year-old husband. Sharon is the one that drives them to their appointments, picks up groceries, and now finds herself unable to drive as the neuropathy in her feet doesn't allow her to feel the car's pedals beneath. Realizing that she would never again be able to drive, she had to sell her car. She didn't feel badly for herself but instead would say, "There is someone always worse off than I am."

Sharon tells me when she goes to the infusion center for her chemotherapy, she sees a five-year-old girl receiving chemo for her ovarian cancer with her mother by her side. She says, "She hasn't even lived yet." Or the young nine-year-old with a brain tumor. Or the twelve-year-old with leukemia. Or the twenty-seven-year-old with melanoma. "They haven't had a chance to live yet," she says.

And so, just as Sharon's lesson to us has helped us respond to this question, "How do these people go on living when they know they are dying?" So, too, does she continue to learn. Her lesson is a tough one. Having always helped others, it was now Sharon's turn to receive the help that they can give her.

Where Do We Go from Here?

Although our individual beliefs support us through this life and take us through the process of dying, my experiences have allowed me to witness a certain commonality that tells me there is a transitional period that takes us all from this life to yet another life.

I encourage you to take time with your loved one and witness for yourselves those behaviors, otherwise uncommon to your loved one but signaling this transition. It may be that they physically reach out with their arms in a seeming hug of recognition of another family member gone before them. They may speak the name of a loved one as though they were able to see them on the other side. Or they may try to physically get up and go, as though on a journey. I ask you to watch for these signs, as it is quite an experience—an honor, actually—to be part of this process.

Now, be aware that there are many out there who feel these uncharacteristic behaviors are the result of being overly medicated, suggesting that their loved one is experiencing visual and auditory hallucinations. But I prefer to believe that this is real. I truly believe that we all go to a place of pure love. I tell my patients it's "love-la-la-land" and it always brings out a smile or a laugh.

So, this transitional period is the stepping-stone to the next life that awaits us, taking us from here on earth to a spiritual place somewhere out there.

Andy, a twenty-seven-year-old cancer patient, requested I be there when he transitioned. What an honor to have been part of his journey from beginning to end. I remember placing my hand on his stomach—his core—when he took his last breath. His grandmother, Marion, spoke these words at that moment. She said, "I feel for those young men and women dying alone out on those battlefields."

How fortunate her grandson was to be surrounded by these loved ones at the time of his transition.

Our Challenge

As much as we are being challenged by our loved ones' diagnosis of cancer, I'd like to challenge each and every one of you, no matter what age or physical condition you find yourselves in, to write your own living will, obituary, and to plan your after events. Your self-designed program could include what you want, who you would like to have speak, the music you would like to hear and the pictures you would want to share about your life. These would be *your* wishes and it would serve as a blessing to your family. Look, we realize how difficult it is already to lose you but knowing that your wishes are being granted adds such meaning to your celebration of life, not to mention saving your family from having to make all those decisions while grieving your loss.

Jillian's father was a very popular singer at his church and before he passed away, he recorded himself singing one of his most favorite hymns. Imagine the impact he had at his own funeral when his voice was heard on the loudspeaker singing this song as the congregation processed out of the church!

A Personal Thank You

I would like to personally thank all those oncologists, doctors, and nurses who care so deeply about their cancer patients. You are all instruments of love and healing. I work right beside you and your commitment and dedication is second to none.

You are indeed living your purpose. Feel your patients' hugs of appreciation. These are bonds that will live on forever.

Epilogue

Many people ask me, "How do you do this kind of work every day? Doesn't it get to you?" The answer is always that I am honored and privileged to be a part of each cancer patient's journey, and part of the comforting, loving, and less painful side on this road.

I also know that when they do leave this cancer journey, through remission or transition, they are no longer suffering. Yes, we do form these very intimate relationships and each one is so very special to me. I would not ever give them less than my best. I treat each one like my own and they can feel that. They teach me the depth of the human spirit as they are always having to dig a little deeper with each new diagnosis, treatment, decision, and hospitalization.

They are the ones who teach me life's lessons. Our conversations are always real, deep, and significant. There are many times when I cry with the cancer patient and that is okay.

There are other times when I simply hold them, and that's okay, too. They need love, they need to be touched and listened to. Sometimes they ask me to speak at their funerals or celebration of life ceremonies. I am once again honored to share their essence with their family and friends. I am so grateful for the deep connection that we make and I believe with all my heart that we will meet again!

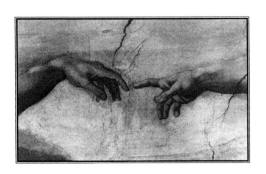

Appendix A
The Benefits of Massage

- Gives comfort and relaxation

- Relieves stress

- Boosts immune system by bringing in new blood, oxygen, and nutrients

- Accelerates the healing process

- Reduces pain by releasing endorphins (natural pain-killers) in the brain and relaxing tight muscles

- Allows a safe space to share feelings and emotions

- Improves sleep by promoting deep relaxation

- Reduces anxiety and depression

- Promotes better digestion by assisting in alleviating constipation and nausea

- Increases energy

- Is non-invasive

Appendix B:
Thoughts and Musings

Some of my patients say that they are actually *glad* to have been diagnosed with cancer as it changes their life for the better. They change what is *trivial* in their life to what is *significant*. They make better decisions for themselves: about their food choices, their friendships, about being okay with setting boundaries and saying *no* when they need to. And they learn the big lessons: how to receive from others, and how to let go of control!

I Believe How You Live is How You Die

If you were always a giving and kind person, you will continue to be that way even during your end stage of life.

If you were always a selfish and controlling person, those ways will follow you as well.

Which way would you choose on the last days of your life? Having witnessed both ways, I can tell you with certainty that being kind is a legacy in itself.

This I Know…

There is so much that I want to teach people through my own experiences in my fifty-one years of living.

I have always felt loved. I thank God and my mother for this. They both taught me how to love—the greatest gift you can give to one another.

From pain comes the biggest lessons.

To let go and truly trust is a daily discipline and will always make you happy. So learn to trust and make room for God's will to be done.

If you are not happy within yourself, you cannot be happy with anyone else in your life.

Stay open and do not be afraid to get hurt. You will discover that people are truly put into your life to teach you.

Listen to your own voice.

I will never understand suffering, especially suffering that I see with cancer. I have learned that **it is not to be understood**.

Family and friends are the most important people in your life.

Relationships don't have to be a struggle. Be honest, communicate, and love.

Extend yourself to others with a smile, a hug, a positive comment, etc. It truly doesn't take a lot of energy! Love is not love unless you put it into action! You have to put something behind it as with anything else in life.

Appreciate everything and everyone in your life…and tell them.

Don't wait until you have a disease or until you are dying.

Say *I love you* often.

Spend time with the people you love.

Balance.

Listen to your "gut." That's where God talks to you.

Listen to your own intuition.

Trust in yourself.

Believe in yourself.

Make a difference in people's lives. That takes some action, time, and love.

Live with no regrets.

Forgive. You may come full circle.

Dispense of your ego.

Exercise your mind, body, and soul.

Be an all-around good person.

Shine your light.

Get into your passions. Your passions are your gifts. This alone will make you happy!

Act in kindness.

Sit alone in stillness.

Share all that you have. That's why you have it!

To-Do List

Healthy

Haircut

Grocery shopping

Child's soccer game

Lunch with friends

Manicure

With Cancer Diagnosis

Looking for wigs, turbans

Driving to yet another doctors appointment

Try to explain your fears to your child

Addressing your own mortality

Surgery

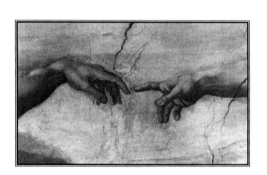

Songs

Just Love

All we have to do
All we have to do
All we have to do
is love
And enjoy the simple things in life
Enjoy the simple things
No past, no future, just now

Why do we get so boggled in the mind and in the
    heart my friends?
Why do we get so boggled in the mind and in the
    heart my friends?

oh, let it go
let it go
and trust

oh, let it go
let it go
and breathe (or let God)

Breathe in all that love
Breathe in all abundance
Breathe out and release the past
And feel, oh feel, the miracles!

It's time to lean on one another
It's time to learn from the pain
And recognize that it's all for our gain
And that these are our precious lessons here on earth

Hurting Heart

When our hearts are sad
Who do we turn to
Do we turn to You
And trust in Your ways

Or do we try
Try to control it
And just get in the way
Get in the way

So why not
Surrender our burdens
And don't take them back
Don't take them back
And just lean on God
For the understanding
Sometimes it's not
For us to understand

So you take that pain
And become a teacher
And hold someone else
Through it too
Just by being there
With a listening ear
You learn compassion
In the deepest way

(by: Denise Morin 2003)

Resource List

www.connectedtouch.org
A charitable, non-profit organization founded by Denise Morin in 2004.

www.dempseycenter.org
The Patrick Dempsey Center for Cancer Hope and Healing, Lewiston, Maine.

www.cancer.org
Global resource for advancing cancer research.

www.oncolink.org
Global resources to cancer-related government sites, hospitals, universities, institutes, medical associations, and foundations.

www.campsunshine.org
On beautiful Sebago Lake in Maine, Camp Sunshine provides respite, support, joy, and hope. FREE to children/families with life threatening illnesses, including an oncology week. Includes 24-hour on-site medical and social support.

www.cancercare.org
Free support to cope with stress, treatments, family issues, etc.

www.cancer.gov/cancertopics/coping
Help with managing physical, emotional, and lifestyle effects. Also includes information on finances and insurance.

www.wikihow.com/write-to-someone-who-has-been-diagnosed-with-cancer
Helpful suggestions on writing a living will.

www.caring.com/obituary-sample
Helpful suggestions on writing an obituary.

About the Author

After earning a bachelor of science from Springfield College in Massachusetts, I attended Downeast School of Massage in Waldoboro, Maine where I received nine months of education in massage therapy. It was on the final day of massage school that I first heard the calling for what I was to do with the rest of my life. At the final practicum, each of us was to massage a preselected individual. All my classmates were given clients from the general public to massage while I was given a client with breast cancer. This was my first experience working with someone with cancer. For some reason, I was not afraid of the person, nor of the word "cancer," so the experience was mutually rewarding.

I then started the first mobile massage business in Maine, bringing my portable table to my clients' homes.

In 2004, I began Connected Touch Inc. (www.connectedtouch. org), a charitable, non-profit organization which provides skilled, supportive touch and massage to cancer patients in their home, hospital, or hospice setting at no fee to them.

As fate would have it, the attorney that helped me become a non-profit was himself a victim of cancer. Incredibly, his bilateral retinal cancer occurred *in utero,* thus rendering him blind since birth. Convinced of Connected Touch's mission, he provided all his time and expertise *pro bono.*

Along with working for Connected Touch, in 2008, I began working part-time as an Oncology Massage Therapist at the Patrick Dempsey Cancer Hope & Healing Center, (www.dempseycenter. org), and at Central Maine Medical Center in Lewiston, Maine.